For Craig Casey

With every good wish —

Mary Ewald

Weapons Against Chaos

Weapons Against Chaos

Mary Ewald

Devin-Adair, Publishers
Greenwich, Connecticut

Copyright © 1986 by Mary T. Ewald

All rights reserved. No portion of this book may be reproduced or transmitted in any form or by any means, electronic or mechanical, including photocopy, recording, or any information storage and retrieval system without the written permission of Devin-Adair, Publishers, 6 North Water Street, Greenwich, Connecticut 06830

Manufactured in the United States of America

First Edition

Library of Congress Cataloging-in-Publication Data

Ewald, Mary T.
  Weapons against chaos.

  I. Title.
PS355.W3W4   1986   811'.54   85-16157
ISBN 0-8159-7225-3

Publisher: C. de la Belle Issue
Managing Director: Roger H. Lourie
Book Design and Production: Arthur Hamparian
Typesetting: Coghill Book Typesetting
Printing: Halliday Litho.

Devin-Adair
Excellence, Since 1911

Contents

Preface   vii

I   *From Mist*   1

Heard Weapons   3
Metamorphoses   4
Soundbirth   6
The Cheetah   7
Summer Rondel   8
Whale Sounds   9
Snow Seurat   11
Concepts of Man   13
The Ascent of Man   14
From Mist   15
The Baghnakh   16
Enchantment   18
Distant Chopin   19
Go, Go False Heart   20
Invidia   21

II   *Snowthreads*   23

Snowthreads   25
The Little Frogs   26
Gorges   27
The Red and the Black   28
New Guinea Feathers   29

Sleeping Venus   30
The Corner   31
Winter Woods   32
For Miliç   33
Rainwood   34
Kick and Claw   35
Medicines   36
Sonnet for Washington, D.C.   37
Scribere Oportet Aqua   38
Εἰμὶ μὲν οὐ φιλόοινος   39
῎Ηδη λευκόϊον θάλλει   40
Ave Atque Vale   41
Unleafing   42
The Mountain Gorilla   43
Sea and Shore Haiku   44
Rhododendron Globes   45

III   *The Knowledge of Relations*   47

Jewels   49
Advice   50
Of Mice and Men   51
Crape Myrtle   52
Autumn Flight   53
After-Images   54
Grass Whiskers   55
Bundle for a Peasant   56
Triangles   57
De Chirico Remembered   58
Heavy-Laden   60
For Piero Della Francesca   61
The Knowledge of Relations   62
Orpheus in Elysium   64
The Horned Owl   67
Odin's Ride   69
Ode for Carved Birds   70

vi

Preface

Mary Ewald, the mother of three sons, is a Harvard PhD in English philology who wrote her thesis on scientific method. Her interest in both the history of words and in science is evident in her verse.

A major theme runs through the poems. The philosophy which dominates twentieth-century thought is the philosophy of language, and her book can be read as a commentary on some of the chief concerns in this body of thought. Each poem is a unit, but the images that embody the theme are repeated (for example, word-bird, fog-drop of water, mathematics-music, snow-snowflake). As soon as one names anything, of course, it immediately becomes a symbol, but when one puts the symbols in different contexts, as in a fugue, the idea, when it recurs, carries meanings it did not have before.

Mary Ewald uses most of the standard verse forms (from that of *Beowulf* to free verse and the sonnet) and images from many times and places in an attempt to underscore the universality of the theme. Chiefly, she says, she uses verse form, like the concept "word," to contrast with formlessness, and she strives for clarity, convinced that obscurity and profundity are not the same thing.

She says she likes to read and to write verse because nothing else creates such a surge and release of emotion while at the same time brandishing so brazen an intellectual weapon against chaos. Of course, mathematics is a sharp tool, carving out the numbers of things, but it is not such an all-inclusive symbolic structure as language. Against evil and confusion, a poem is not worthless. People need to think, and they must think in words.

–Richard Wilbur

I

From Mist

Heard Weapons

Hugging the marsh beside the river the herons
Reared a slender bill to swallow, then laid
One long leg akimbo and began to wade,
Leaving their footprints in mud in unseen chevrons.
Floating the sky over the canyon the falcons
Stretched their slender wings and flew unafraid
Between ribbons of cloud crisscrossed into braid,
Forging no permanent marks with their waving pinions.
Defining light-years, speech reverberates,
Sending small messages pulsing cunningly caged
In a lonely semaphore that penetrates
By sound and symbol the nebulous region of word:
Poems, in the battle with changing armors waged
Against chaos and old night, weapons heard.

Metamorphoses
(for Roland Barthes and Ferdinand de Saussure)

Striking his golden lyre, Orpheus sings
His words and woos Eurydice. Without one care,
The young girl walks through pliant grasses
Swept in sunlight. On her bridal day,
Like spring itself she moves, with all
Her maids-in-waiting about her, until by chance
She treads upon a snake. Lissom, but pierced
By venom, she trips and falls, stumbling
Into death. Hymen's torch flickers
And burns out in coiling smoke that fills
The eye with tears, with iridescent
Water-drops.

         So Orpheus sang
Aloud his loss on earth. Then, in pursuit, barely
Breathing, he descended deep between the gates
Of Hades into that desert where the shades
Exist immortal; dead and lifeless is the kingdom
Ruled by Pluto with Persephone, condemned
Because she had eaten six pomegranate seeds.
"My mission is to find Eurydice," Orpheus moans
In Hades, "Eurydice, a girl whose thoughts were innocent,
"Yet she tripped upon a serpent, and her short walk
"Was done. Unless she comes back with me
"To earth—I love her so—I think
"I'll stay in Hell."

             All Hades weeps.
Even the rulers of number and death are touched
By music and promise to give him his Eurydice.
Through fog and drifting shadows, the singer
Will have to mount to light; through the twists
Of Tartarus, the sinuous paths wind long
That climb to earth and life. In that infernal storm
The warring winds which never rest lead lovers
Like cranes that go chanting their calls, making a long
Streak of themselves in thin air. Just as Lot's wife,
Because she looked back when fleeing wicked
Sodom's waste, melted precipitate into
A pillar of salt, so too Orpheus must not look
Behind. A named meaning is a dead meaning.
He cannot escape the world of signs, yet he must not
Kill what he has symbolized.
Stalwart, he holds tight the small hand, walks
With Eurydice, and feels her trembling. Too soon,
Alas, he reaches out to touch her shade;
Too soon he turns around in the dense atmosphere.
Eurydice, because of touch and turn and look,
Dissolves into the impermeable dark. Once more,
In the milky mist, Orpheus tries to embrace
The world of emptiness. In vain. On earth now,
Like Ceres in all that pain, alone, listening
To Orpheus' lays, there are the trees, the birds,
The rocks.

               Orpheus' looking back
Did not kill Eurydice. The snake did.

Soundbirth

After the clang of the morning tympani
The snow fell down on Christmas Day
So soft, like—suddenly I heard—
Sound, strains remembered, streaming the chorus
Of the Bach Mass, singing out clear as distant bells
Ringing, winging feathered, *Et incarnatus est,*
Each note of the melody congealed
In the minor mode, pebbles of resonance frozen
Single, each note of the music
Hanging like icicles in a line
Till, still, each earring of ice, iridescent,
Its chain of overtones dangling transparent,
Frozen water pendent, then melted,
Pelted, dropping another note
To glisten in its own snowfall,
Snowflakes drifting wild, moist fleece,
Benign the rime
In snowslip sliding, the flurry firn,
White hoarfrost, milk flowing light,
The note, the ball, will fall.

The Cheetah

I recall how frightened I was when I was small
And read the first time the words of Heraclitus
That I could not place a stick in the same stream's fall
Twice: there is no return to a past to delight us.
I remember the sadness in Horace's great lyric
When he promised to erect in his odes a document
Whose words would endure longer as a panegyric
Than the mass of molten brass in a monument.
And Shakespeare's insubstantial pageant?——of late
I no longer fear what leaves no rack behind,
But rather hate the photograph, the date,
All things that reduce the free into the lined:
I'm like a cheetah chasing what's alive,
Since I know whatever does not move is dead.

Summer Rondel

Around the horizon the sun threw a rim of gold
Where beneath thick clouds there stretched a lapis sea
That was dappled by light as far as the eye could see.

The yellow band was a hoop that was twisting bold,
Like a wheel that has turned with the wind from weather to
    lee.
Around the horizon the sun threw a rim of gold
Where beneath gray clouds there stretched a lapis sea.

The hand of the sun drew the blue into its fold
And caressed the water wherever its rays would be:
There each small wave was dancing its wave-dance free.
Around the horizon the sun threw a rim of gold
Where beneath stray clouds there stretched a lapis sea
That was dappled by light as far as the eye could see.

Whale Sounds

(For Jacques Cousteau and Noam Chomsky)

The baby whale stretched a formless hulk
Breaking the blue of the infinite sea,
Still dependent for food on his mother's milk
And too young to know how to sound with his bulk.

The engines circled his random play,
The motorboats curled and surrounded his sport,
They lost his hearing in random coils
Of sound that confounded his frolicsome way.

The frogmen leaped down from their stations to dive,
They tagged the back of the baby sperm,
Then set him adrift to go back to his school
Of whales that awaited his return alive.

And the divers went back to their mother boat,
They took off their wet gear by the lights of the hold,
They took up their ledgers more precious than gold,
They returned to their task among men who float.

And they talked in tones mysterious and low,
They discussed the wild ways of the whales of the sea,
They talked of migrations as strange as could be,
They were joined on a voyage of Jacques Cousteau.

And the waves of their words pulsed the universe-sea
As the sounds of the men joined the sounds of the whales;
And all together were recorded in time,
And all were true and will always be.

For the word that means is the word that has been,
All words that are ripples in someone's throat,
The pulses that come from each tiny boat
And spread trickles on the face of a watery screen.

So tell your professor of philology,
Who studies the sounds in the animal sea
Which gambol and sport on a limitless spree
Swimming languages roaming so free:

He who opens his mouth and tells all the tales
Is one who will sound to eternity;
And it's a fact of being, of ontology,
There could be no whale-talk, ever, without whales.

Snow Seurat

How dense the dots of snow are falling down,
Swirling, curving, twirling all around,
Blanketing tree and bush and fence and ground——

Seurat's painted specks, like snowflakes, fall,
Covering a canvas universe wide and tall,
Posing between the eye and the world a wall:

Seen near the window, small snow dots are wild,
Dancing irregular, free—but ordered, piled
In clockwork blocks before the pine tree, filed,

Composed, each flake equidistant, ruled
In graphs, descending geometrically schooled,
Believing its destiny released, but fooled,

Drawn down to earth by gravity at last,
Clinging to its view that the other flakes are massed,
But it can whirl and turn and sing and blast,

Floating sinuous; yet it is watching chained
Like all the other flakes that are moving laned,
Drawn by some mysterious artist and waned

From power—only the individual dot
From out the vast, conglomerate, inchoate lot
Calibrated unique, daubed on its own spot.

Quiet, lone, each one snowflake is resting
As it watches the other flakes moving about, testing
Their own place in the pointillist painting, questing.

Behind the snowing, in back of the countless brushstrokes,
The eye composes its picture of ashes and hemlocks,
Snowflakes forming all roads and houses and rocks.

Composed in Seurat's brushwork dreamworld of snow
A painted harlequin is hatted, sounding his horn,
Masterful amid the points——blow, clown, blow!

Concepts of Man

Rocking and cuddling, cooing my best,
I hold my baby upon my breast
Trying as well as ever I can
To see in him the concepts of man.
What will he be? A Renaissance
Figure, exerting a varied puissance
Upon a real world extending high
And low, from hell up to the sky,
Guest of a mid point of God's seeing
Infinity in the Great Chain of Being,
A little higher than the beasts
Consuming, below, their knowledgeless feasts,
But held down by natural antiphonals
To a spot a bit beneath the angels?
Or is he born, as John Locke said,
A *tabula rasa,* nothing in his head,
An eighteenth-century design, a naked
Reasoner, at least when the crooked
Customs of barbarous ages come off
And all superstitious ideas are doffed?
Or perhaps a twentieth-century creature,
Blind matter's newest feature,
An animal surely, but one transfigured
By language and mathematics conjured
By chance in long eons of time
Or evolved through the struggle to survive in slime?
One more problem to be left up above
While I see him here as the one I love.

The Ascent of Man

The monstrosities of nude primitive man
Tearing the beating hearts out of the chests
Of their victims, holding them dripping as high as they can,
Cruel hands covered with gore at their idol's behests.
Medieval mobs hooting and shouting,
Massing their timbers and beating on hollow drums,
Proclaiming the triumph of hooded heretics' routing
In fire, each torture added in heaven's sums.
Grim modern man trudging by millions in cold lines
Of armies and prisons and labor camps, too late
To rebel against the unmistakable signs
Of his sacrifice to the glory of the state.
The atomic scientist contemplating on his knees
The mushroom cloud of Mephistopheles.

From Mist

Undulating around the bamboo stalks,
The filmy mist settles down in a sheet of gray
Which stirs without quickening and quietly walks
Around the promontory at the edge of the bay
Until it meets the glaze of the water shivering
So still it bears no ripples but rather shakes
Congealed like a bowl of dark dense jelly, quivering
As it rubs against the edge of the land and takes
Its mouthfuls of leaf and bites of dry raw reed,
Each reed jutting knifelike and pointed, each leaf
Cutting the fog with its rapier edges filigreed
By small drops of water etched on each blade's sheaf:
Out of the cool of the silvery grisaille rise
The lighted candles of several fireflies.

The Baghnakh

Late afternoon glow was washing the pink
City of Jaipur in shades of rose and apricot
While bathing the rugged hills with gold
When you and I returned from riding
Those elephants. I recall mounting the stationary
Steps so that I could climb onto the *howdah*
And then clinging to my skirt, trying to keep
It down so that too much leg wouldn't
Show. I held my narrow dress and rocked with the ambling
Gait of the elephant, dusty gray in the hot
Sun, the deepest wrinkles in his skin,
The deepest wrinkles I had ever seen,
And his feet were padded, making his
Movement silent even though it jerked
Like an old film when the projector is also
Not new. We rode them, you your elephant
And I mine, to the Amber Palace, which stretched
Atop the long dry plain like a patch of petals
Fallen scattered from a dusty rose. It was made of
Red clay, of pink sandstone inlaid with white
Marble, its windows of lace filigreed with flowers,
Itself a flower. You could imagine the women
Of the harem inside clad in silk saris, red and blue
And yellow and green, always trimmed in shining
Gold, ordering their servants to bring the jewelry box.
Within the walls were everything a Rajput
Prince required: a fort, a palace, a temple,
A lake, and, once, a garden. The stream had dried
Up, but we had to think about its running through

The pavilion, sighing softly, while hot scented
Breezes flowed from far-away hills, wind rippling edges
Of silk garments. All those piercing turrets, all those arched
Balconies embellished with carved screens. Yes, it was
Floral, but the flowers were without their inner
Heart, no stamens, no pistils, just the dried and crumpled
Petals. While we were returning to the hotel we looked
Back at the cracked earth surrounding the walled
City and it was as though gashed by a nailed
Tiger's claw, a gigantic *baghnakh,* that ancient
Steel glove sharp enough to slash through chain mail
And tear up a man's beating chest. At the hotel
We ate amid the modern whisperings and plottings,
The new Palace of the Winds, the final decaying
Of the Rajput warriors, the shadows falling across
White tablecloths, the waiters scurrying
Between East and West, their brown faces sweating
Beneath enormous turbans colored saffron, cinnabar,
Marigold, peacock. The mysteries and opulence
Of the long line of maharajahs ended here
In an air-conditioned dining room, but it was the heat
That brought out the scarlet flowers of the *gol mohurs,*
The flames of the forest. Each face in the room was reflected
In small mirrors, thousands of them—I thought I saw
My face in one—each face distorted and gnarled
And weathered like the elephant, like the savage
Hills beyond the city walls, each face seeing in
Small mirrors the tell-tale petals wrinkling.

Enchantment

The world of enchantment—the fountains flowing
Between the colored stones inlaid of the Turkish harem.

At Versailles, along the green *allées,* the marble statues
    white and cold
Reflected manifold in mirrors framed in gold.

Behind the blossoms from mist on the Japanese screen
The silk damask stirred by the wind's soft blowing.

Bright light falling filtered and patterned
Through Brussels lace, gleaming polished on silver and brass.

The intricacy of carving in the medieval cloister,
Its dancing of piers and frets and mullions in stone.

Nothing is lovelier than to look into your face,
Its perfection of eye and hair and bone.

Distant Chopin

The sound came through the door clearly
Though from far away in another corner
Of the house, having climbed the stairs
And crossed the hall, lingering just a moment
In the dining room beneath the chandelier,
Flowing across the red velvet carpet
Lying like moss between the banks of books
Stretching long lengths of library shelves,
Music streaming out of the cracks in the varnish
Wrinkling the mahogany of the grand piano—
The trills of Chopin, flickering like butterfly wings,
Dancer's feet fluttering in *entrechat,*
The waterfall rippling before the tolling of the bell:
The hesitation and, suddenly, melody.

Go, Go, False Heart

Go, go, false heart, escape from my true fears
    Go faster yet, oh quickly, race away
Hear no heavy part my music hears
      Fear masters all from night to day
          Fall cones and leaves
          Wild winds weave
          Nude trees grieve
          Oh I could yet
On his love my own is set
        Fall, fall, fall, fall
Still I would not pay him with my debt

Invidia

(For George Borrow)

Imagine how it would feel to be the great
Alexander astride Bucephalus
Charging, afraid only to be born too late
To find enough gallant new worlds to conquer;
Conceive his raising high his left arm, slow,
Then slicing the Gordian knot at one sword's blow.

Consider how it must have been when Einstein
First heard the music that sounds to frontiers of spheres
Dangling serene on their rich rational line
Caressed in the laws of relativity,
Discordant theorems slain by his drive to select
A perfect melody with his great intellect.

Think of Shakespeare's power to move men's souls
Through the play of life by characters meshed in plots,
Making each lightning word serve dramatic goals
As it bursts crackling across the curtained sky,
Quick rivers of flame which startle, manifold,
Their explosions flooding the labyrinth with gold.

Splendid in beauty, blonde Helen of Troy
Walked the ramparts of the citadel alone,
Stepping those tremors in loins of each man and boy
That dance like waves on water, ripple-fingered,
Sparkling undulate, softness uncontrolled,
The echoes of loveliness pulsing through ages untold.

To be like St. Francis so consumed by love
That he went out to face the mad beast of Gubbio:
"My brother Wolf, make peace with God above,"
And, lo, he felt in his hand an animal paw,
All things great and little becoming eavesdroppers
Of one who preached to small birds and even grasshoppers.

No envy inhabit the eye that is able to see,
But decree, "Rapture sets my heart on fire,"
I'm alive to the miracle that life can be,
Praising the God of creation with that Romany
Without sight or limbs, who still wished for life knowing
He could feel whenever the wind on the heath was blowing.

Gorges

Erupting, the fiery heart of the active volcano,
A mountain drunk on Polynesian kava,
Ignited fireworks in fountains from its inferno,
Its crevices running hot with molten lava;
The northeast wind lashed the sea into a fury,
Huge walls of water rearing to devour the land,
Its power subsiding only when it blew itself weary,
Waves leaving behind scalloped foam in lace on the sand;
The thunderhead rolled majestic, a giant lyre,
Its lightning pulsing so brilliant the whole earth winked
As the sky became a river of crackling fire
Where before in the heavens small stars in multitudes
    blinked;
Nothing on the earth or the sea or the sky above
Grander than a gorge of hate that explodes into love.

The Red and the Black

When Carmen stands handcuffed outside the cigarette
Factory singing exultantly, "Free I shall die,"
In the Habañera flaunting her charms as coquette
While striding the stage for the men of Seville who sigh
Vying to prove that for every woman who is tough
A male waits ready in weakness to worship her;
When she scorns Don José, his manhood gone, with the
    rough
Words, "We are finished," in futile efforts to deter
The knife of jealousy which will carve out its revenge,
Rising like the strings in a loud nasal crescendo;
Choosing to live her few hours wild, does she challenge
The corrida with her petty lurid imbroglio?
Or is it the composer who in her last gypsy breath
Warns how close love is both to war and to death?

New Guinea Feathers

Spreading his pinions and fanning his delicate tail,
The bird of paradise waxes in his display;
Head flashing yellow and green, resplendent, male,
He touches his beak to the wings of his mate as she lay.
Leaping are the shadows flickering in the jungle night,
Gleaming the ebony skin, the ivory teeth,
Flowing the feathered headdress twirling light,
In the sing-sing whirling, used bow and arrow in sheath.
Sensitive the lens of the curious camera eye
Capturing the movement of the natives exploding in dance,
Recording the swirl of the past as it vanishes by
For all to see, and killing it by its glance,
Bird, man, film, ephemeral as the fuzz
On the globe of the peach—still, this beauty was.

Sleeping Venus

Giorgione's Sleeping Venus lies
Nude, one arm with its elbow
Bent as a pillow for her head,
Its hair of autumn hue,
Her left leg extended,
Covering the right foot,
Her other arm long, sinuous,
Its hand curved to the vee
Between her legs. Languid,
Breathing softly, she rests,
The rocks, the trees, the landscape
Scene bathed in golden
Light. Tawny the crevices,
Russet the draperies
On which she sleeps. Today
A few leaves, gold and brown,
Like a hand, are hiding
The secret parts of the forest.

The Corner

Tell it to the men at the corner,
    Whisper it to every lass,
I have seen the face in the mirror,
    Felt the breath on the glass.
Whatever heaves to a climax
    Will tremble and pass,
The rush of the wave on the sand,
    Of the wind in the grass.

Winter Woods

North wind shaking tree limbs bare as bone
Beneath, leaves rolling dry and crumpled brown
But never walk the winter woods alone

Stirring branches will make their wretched groan
Gray boughs are nude without a summer gown
North wind shaking tree limbs bare as bone

Summer music has turned to solemn moan
Barren the woods from tangled root to crown
But never walk the winter woods alone

The sun bleak white behind clouds gray as stone
Showers of russet leaves now tumbling ground
North wind shaking tree limbs bare as bone

Tired needles dripping, brown the pine tree's cone
Nothing is hidden, every secret known
But never walk the winter woods alone

Bits of fallen branch tips lying prone——
Beware the heavy skies before they drown
North wind shaking tree limbs bare as bone
But never walk the winter woods alone

For Miliç

Today I learned you had a return of your sickness,
The canker eating the heart from the bloom of the rose,
The scythe that reaps in a path which constantly grows,
Leaving in its place torn petals and ooze and thickness.
Today I cleaned all my rings and held them up
To the light, watching them glisten in the beams of the sun
While casting bright prisms as fast as their gleams could run,
Afraid that a blow might shatter their flooding cup.
Today I heard the pianist matching his frothing
Notes to the rhythms and beats of the orchestra playing
The D Minor Concerto of Brahms, its vast themes saying
The beauty of sweet sound living. There is nothing
More magical, disappearing dreamlike and fragile,
Than music that echoes and sings but a little while.

Rainwood

The rain stretches long in sheets
Like paper with vertical lines,
Soaking whatever it meets,
Turning needles down on the pines.

Whatever can run now flees,
And the woodpecker stops his pecks,
Since even the wood of the trees
Looks soggy as in old shipwrecks.

Kick and Claw

Kick and claw, then bare the teeth and bite,
Scratch, nails red, to the top of the churning heap,
Nothing can be achieved without a fight,
So prepare your stomach to ignore its nauseous leap;
Ranting and raving, surmount the humbler types,
Since power alone is the consummation of life;
Blazon the victory, open wide the pipes
Proclaiming the victim supine beneath the knife;
The passage of man lies underneath the dark
Shadow of mindless eternity consuming its past
Fast, sere, steering clear, removing stark,
Blotting the individual beneath its vast
Footsteps that forward, crushing, relentless tread
Dead, where nonetheless the martyrs bled.

Medicines

Better than amphetamines
Beauty lifts the spirits
And makes a full heart sing,
But nothing cracks one's bones
And sets the ears to ring
Like conscious cruelty,
More bitter than strychnine.

Sonnet for Washington, D.C.

Blue sky floods pink as dusk is easing down,
A few cirrus clouds trailing red streaks like hair
And catching the glow from the sun, as in the still air
The silver arc of the plane soars up from the ground
Gliding above the vistas of Washington's town.
The Capitol dome with its windows myriad, fair,
Reflects the sunset like a bonnet made to wear
With its long shawl of a Mall which wraps around
Green to the President's house, a rectangle of white;
The Doric columns of Lincoln's marble shrine
Across the calm Potomac waters shine
With Jefferson's, all lines threading the needle
Piercing black velvet in the fading light——
America's city stretches jewelled, necklaced in night.

Scribere Oportet Aqua
(Translated from Catullus)

No one—says my own mistress—can gain wedlock with her
    charms
    But me, though the god Jupiter seek her for mate.
So she talks. But I surmise, what a woman declares to her
    lover
    Ought to be writ in the wind, writ in the flowing water.

Εἰμὶ μὲν οὐ φιλόοινος

(From the Greek Anthology)

Surely, little maid of mine,
I do not indulge in wine,
Yet whenever you aspire,
Ruby drink I should desire,
First you touch the ample cup,
And I shall take your offer up.
When you press it with the tips
Of your dainty puckered lips,
Then no longer I with ease
Can be as sober as I please,
Or persuade my wavering soul
To flee the sweetly flowing bowl
Since the cup conveys from you
Prizes which I think my due,
Bringing to this heart enraptured
Kisses which from you it captured.

῞Ηδη λευκόϊον Θάλλει

(From the Greek Anthology)

Already the white violet is blooming
With mountain-roaming lilies; the pale narcissus
Has opened up its head that loves the mists.
Yet the choicest bud of all the flowers that grow
Is one I call my own Zenophila
More seductive she is by far than any rose.
O meadows, how can you smile and so foolishly
Toss to the breeze your gleaming, golden tresses?
Can you not see that this young maid of mine
Outshines in beauty all your fresh new garlands
Vying to shed their fragrance in the wind?

Ave Atque Vale

    (From Catullus, in the original Latin meter)

Tossed over many an ocean and guided through many a
    nation,
    By your tomb, my brother, I stand. Painful precedents cry
Out now that I give you the last sad rites of the lifeless.
    Vainly to you I speak; vainly mute ashes reply.
Nonetheless, since the goddess of fortune has taken you from
    me,
    Wretched brother of mine, snatched you unseasonably,
Here, in accord with the ancient traditions of our forefathers
    That have been handed down, sad propriety,
Know of my weeping with brotherly tears for him I loved well:
    Into eternity, hail and one last farewell.

Unleafing

After the rains every trunk and every twig
Have become so dark, so blackened with wet
That anyone can see and understand
The architecture of each tree.

Especially the maples have
Gnarled, twisted branches
Hung with pronged gold leaves,
Sometimes tinged with red, clustered
And swaying now in the winds
After the storm, which scatter
The leaves on the ground,
Sending them scurrying
Across the green lawn, green
As only autumn grass is green,
Deep green, cold green, dotted
Now with maple gold.

And the heads of the trees
Toss and bend, wending the huge
Golden flakes twisting,
Sailing them into lakes.

Nothing so gold as gold
Maples leaving yellow puddles
Of leaves on green lawns,
Sunny trees unleafing,
Sheaves in a gold reef.
Brief.

The Mountain Gorilla

    (For Adrien Deschryver)

I like the white man who calls me Kasimir.
I know he's watching as I lead my gorilla family
Across the new road they've built through my jungle in Zaire.
I stand at the crossroads. I look up and down carefully
Until the women and the children, the bachelor males
Have passed the cut quickly and hidden safe in the trees.
We've a long journey—I hear the young ones' wails.
It's hard, getting enough bamboo to eat, on your knees.
Why, to feed myself takes sixty pounds a day.
That man tracking with two Pygmies behind the rest . . . .
Does he want to see my young ones grow strong as they play?
Is he friend or foe? I'd best bare my lips, beat my chest,
My inadequate defense against guns and camera eyes.
I've grown to know the ambivalent nature of spies.

Sea and Shore Haiku

Andrew Marvell said
He wanted to banish all
That's ever been made

Into a green thought
In a green shade, but for me
Personally, I'd

Rather gather what's
Wrought into the azure play
Of a clear blue day!

Rhododendron Globes

Your head upon my shoulder, breathing deep,
Regular, every muscle, every nerve
Relaxed, lying flushed in my arm's curve,
Unfettered, lax, and smiling in your sleep,
Every shadow now vanished that tries to creep
Between the male animal and his verve,
All cares resolved, abandoned to the swerve
That made those dots of sweat that beaded steep
The crevices which on your forehead lie,
Glistening warm and moist before they die.
I recall the breeze that blew from off the coves
Of Montauk once and swept the room we'd filled
With rhododendron blooms, the windows spilled
With red and mauve and purple bursting globes.

III

The Knowledge of Relations

Jewels

I stood within an emerald one spring
And saw the forest's dancing green afloat,
Where every new leaf shimmered, as in a ring
The darts of light within the jewel's throat.
I watched the flakes of snow fall softly down
Mantling the earth with a lustrous, shining swirl
Which adorned the fields like an iridescent crown
And turned the world into a giant pearl.
I ran on the beach when waves were dashing high
Their beads of foam a radiance set on fire,
Casting bright prisms growing arced in the sky
While the sea lay sparkling blue, a giant sapphire.
The diamond sun refracts for each man's sight
Rich rainbow hues of God's own one white light.

Advice

My dear, sitting there, legs crossed,
Lipstick pink, every hair in place,
No one by make-up is going to be fooled,

Too much regularity is fake——
All your strenuous efforts merely waste——
Furthermore tasteless, like a store-bought cake.

Much more aesthetic is what is living,
Artifice can't take the place of giving,
And beauty is never machine-tooled.

Of Mice and Men

God was throwing universes around
For sport, tossing them high, bouncing them down,
Practicing in turn His windup, His slow ball, His fast,
His various sorts of curves from first to last,
Causing all things to circle from rose to star,
From nebulae to corpuscles scattering afar
His spirals, twining everything growing with traction,
Whirling worlds ajar in every fraction
Of space, His arm like a giant repeating gun
Firing bullets bursting in air, for fun,
Hooking bows, carving arches, with spoon
Shots pitching in festoons from snail to moon,
Sphering projectiles in crescents, in heavenly larks
Sending His globes coning in circles and arcs,
From volcanic clefts to diffraction patterns on the face
Of green beryl twirling every atom in lace.

How very serene the ship of the universe tacks
In the empyrean, the music measured from the cracks
Of the star dust, no end of planets for sails,
No end of suns for motors to follow sky trails,
As God's toy boat floats the paths of His indigo sea.
"But something," God says, "is not, it seems to Me,
"Quite right—problems for a microscopic eye,
"Which I'll have to attend to assuredly by and by—
"In the hold of my cruising vessel, those mice and men
Are gnawing a crack I must patch. And I'll say when."

Crape Myrtle

On a summer's day the little children play
The old familiar games that tightly link
Like hands the generations, then give way
Their scores to laughter and in the soft grass sink.

I watch the fluffy clouds go sailing by
Skating flowers into a welkin rink:
The crape myrtle is throwing rockets into the sky
Red and mauve and watermelon pink.

Autumn Flight

Flying high above trees and houses and halls,
Here and there a section of those who have made it
Flaunting a pool to swim in and holes for golf balls,
That must avoid the sand traps of the course as men laid it;
Looking over cold water curving in coves
At the dots of white boats, their beaks bobbing the blue,
Huddled shaking close together in droves
These last days of summer when the sea gulls are few;
Blocks of houses spreading in rectangles and squares,
Each cube the dwelling of someone individual,
Stretched on a graph of mathematical lairs,
Braving the gnawing of raw chaos residual;
A bit of color where a few old leaves blanch,
Of yellow crying out against the gray branch.

After-Images

After the blood has rushed away from the lips,
Among the myriad things which I have seen
Are visual after-images purple and green
Of the sheaf of a knife-blade enameled moist to the tips.
Among all the azaleas speckled red and white
Every chalice lies open, petalled, proclaiming its stamen,
Each bush in the garden hanging flower-laden,
Teeming with odors languishing rich in sunlight.
Among all the sounds of the instruments making their
    music,
Opening their throats and spreading their joyous song,
Stretching the chain of the melody striding along
Threading the warp of its polychromatic fabric,
Among all the things I have seen and heard and felt,
Nothing lovelier than the man with whom I've dwelt.

Grass Whiskers

The heaven is closed in, gray, opaque and heavy,
And rhododendron leaves are curled up tight;
Like a rag doll's head, the branches of weeping cherry
Lean wisps of uncombed hair in the morning light.

The yellow that glows behind the black pine stalks
Is all that there is of dawn in a wintry sky
As the last dead leaves are scattering rusty and browned,
Clustering in bushes, decaying along the ground.

Matted and stiff, the dried up grasses lie
In knots that freckle the worn-out face of the lawn;
Before the flakes of snow will tumble and spawn,
An old black crow, on the stubble, waddles by.

Bundle for a Peasant

Here on his native New England soil returned,
Clutching his quivers of laurels new-won with his pen,
Wearing his garlands of new-mastered customs, alien,
Having left behind America's distances churned
By their lack of exact degree, Henry James turned
And looked outside his father's window, his ken
Fixed on the green lying soft beyond the fen:
Glancing up he saw a man walking and spurned
With precision his vision of "a peasant carrying faggots"——
A poor man striding simply, beyond the pale
Of the classes, living earth-caked beneath his divots.
Before James, the poet had joined with the statesman to hail
The farmers who with rude starred banners unfurled
Stood up and fired the shots heard round the world.

Triangles

Where is the Arab rosary I put
Away, thinking the golden color would match
The gold in the crown of the Peruvian Virgin shut
In her timeless perfection of pyramids that catch
Their rhythms from the shape of the babe who staring sits
Above the lace of the ruffle which garlands her hand,
Its flowers repeating the flowers of the dress which fits
The shape of her face and stiffly, band on band,
Falls forked, oblique, with all the lines the lines
Of the aquiline eyes, which by pairs form the focal cusp
Of a painting in space measured by elbow signs,
All things triangular in this one woman's clasp?
Where is the caliper to probe the temporal
And grasp the mathematics of truth archetypal?

De Chirico Remembered

There's a spot in the forest where the woods divide,
Where the dense path veers and turns toward the light
Opening spacious and wide;

In this gap that stretches beyond the bend
One sees in a vista, through the green,
To the classical arch at its end.

The arch is white and is made of marble,
And the steps leading up to the marble are double,
While the openings in the arch are three.

And up to the top of the arch climbs a stair,
The steps climb up on the left and the right,
They climb partly out of sight.

As they climb, the steps wind to the crest of the arch,
They swerve like two bending wings, in a curve,
Floating like the wings of a bird.

And the steps to the crown of the arch are railed,
Each rail being spaced in a regular scale,
And each carved pale stands free.

As the rail winds up to the tip of the stairs,
The rail climbs skyward curling in pairs:
Then it rolls over the marble arch.

And the land lies level around the marble,
Flat, it reaches the arched curvature,
Its green surrounding the white

In all the varied shades of verdure,
And the green is dark and the green is clean
In cunning shades of citrine;

But this green casts shadows of a deeper color,
The shadows of the trees are not green at all,
They glow with a darker tremor.

The spectres of the sky the scene overreach,
They turn, they burn, with a translucent sheen,
And the color of the sky is peach.

A riderless horse walks into the set,
A riderless horse with no mount to net
His coat of pure shining white.

The hooves of the horse move stately and slow,
Rhythmic and majestic, in a straight line they go,
Each hoof is raised in its turn.

And the hooves as they tread shine gleaming and clean,
They shine as clean as though washed in a stream,
They walk but they make no sound.

The riderless horse has paced into space——
As he marches, in the light, he shines milky white,
His mane coruscates like silk.

He tramps with his mane flowing white as milk;
He treads in grace through the green and the light;
He marches toward the classical arch.

And the saddle on the back of the horse is clean,
Its leather gleaming polished and bright,
And the stirrups are hanging loose.

The stirrups hang loose on the horse and are dangling,
On his sinewy flanks, the stirrups are jangling,
The sunlight sparkles them silver,

As the reins hang loose from his neck and are pending,
As the reins hang loose on the white horse withers,
They float in the wind like ribbons.

Heavy-Laden

Heavy the skies hang low
Thick like cotton fleece,
Heavily they hang.

Heavy the wind sings long
Wailing its weary lay,
Wearily it sang.

Heavy the gait of the donkey
Trudging with its dragging feet,
Weary its pace.

Heavy she sits on the beast
Bearing her weary burden,
Heavy her face.

Heavy the steps of the guide
Leading his bride on her mount,
Weary the while.

Light the coo of the babe
Newborn in the manger stall,
Light His smile.

For Piero Della Francesca
    The *Nativity* Angels

But one bird perched on the roof held up by sticks
As in front of its parallelogram dotted with sod,
Casting an oblique shadow on the manger of bricks,
Five tall angels sing out the glory of God.
Carolling barefoot in front of the ox and the ass,
Plucking the strings of two golden, pear-shaped lutes,
Mouths frozen open, stayed by the sounds as they pass,
They listen, expressions withdrawn as though they are mutes,
Calm, unearthly still, on columnar molds
Their blue robes falling in shades of lapis ruth,
Eyes burning, turned in on the vision that unfolds
In every drawn line its asymptote of truth:
A harmony in ovals proclaims aloud the surd
Majesty of infinite music unheard.

The Knowledge of Relations

Myself, I've always loved from the first minute
The dialogues of Plato, longed to escape the cave,
And all my heroes in philosophy have taken
The rational line. I like Descartes, and I like
Leibnitz, leading, as they do, straight to Kant.
Mathematical logic is no surprise to me
Since I've always suspected that knowledge
That makes ripples, the only sort worth anything,
Can only be knowledge of relations. So last night
At the concert, just after the Mozart Serenade,
When you walked into the other side of the hall,
We did not bow, or wave, or speak, but our eyes
Met. I know it and you know it
And the spark went flying like a shooting star
In a black sky, and so what do you call it,
Across the light-years of our severed worlds,
That one second of blue-white comunication?

Orpheus in Elysium

    Non temer, chè il nostro passo
    Non ci può torre alcun: da tal n'è dato

Orpheus, singing, Eurydice lost, took time
To reveal the aspects of himself in succession.
Standing between two mirrors facing each other,
He watched in both an infinite progression.
Whether he looked before or behind, right or left,
He felt himself a machine, an automaton filled
With clichés and chattering away, lonely, to itself.
Language, he thought, means nothing: it's a mere
Computer's symbolic gesture flagging down
The void. In reality, there is no soul, no God,
No fate, no ego, no grandeur, and no meaning.
From energy, particles precipitate like raindrops
From a cloud.

Bemoaning Eurydice, Orpheus taught the men of Thrace
To make love to boys; the sign-snake that bites
Eurydice destroys the holy family. Compelling art, too, is
Bereft; it knows no value, only gesture. More
Memorable than the gift is the package; the medium
Is the message. How trivial the murmurs of the voice;
Chaotic mist is lashed with the strife of winds.
In his songs, Orpheus now voyages, not like Ulysses,
Sails spread, rigging taut, to discover
Immortal beauty, but to find the solipsistic point
Where meaning finally vanishes in Hell.

                    Enraged, ignored, a crowd of angry
Women stand up and toss their spears aimed at Orpheus'
          mouth.
Above the poet's music, the clattering noise of life
Unexamined loops its bloodthirsty way. Just as a stag,
Wounded, is put to death by dogs, so the barbarous
Maenads surround the signifier. His sides whipped by
          branches
Stripped from trees, the creator they stone, they beat,
They smear with hardened clay. Yet still the poet
Breathes in song. His critics seek deadlier weapons
And grab willy-nilly from farmers' fields horns
Torn from heads of oxen. Against animal wrath, Orpheus
Begs for mercy; the multitude refuses. Exhausted,
With one last breath, Orpheus' shade escapes and weaves
Invisibly in waves of air.

                    All earth was
Songless. The saddened birds, the rocks, the trees,
The very smallest stones, sobbed loud for Orpheus.
Dismembered arm from shoulder, knee from thigh
His scourged body lay. Hebrus, the river, caught his head
And lyre: lapped in the curling waves, his dead tongue
Still sang and singing floated down to Lesbos.

                    Salt spray in his hair, Orpheus' head
Faced upward on strange sands. There a wild snake coiled to
          pierce
His lips and eyes, to strike. Apollo was quicker.
Beginning, middle, end is three. Reality is in mind,
In nature, and in the word, but only their signs are
Eternal. As the serpent's fangs flickered, the god
With one glance turned it into polished stone and as a stone
The snake stayed, smiling, open-jawed.

                    The myth had been
Fulfilled. At last the poet's soul, free, stepped down
From earth to Hades to walk the places it already
Knew; and there it felt its way toward Elysium,

The beautiful. In symbols the inchoate struggles
Into form when Orpheus, the prince of peace, embraces
Eurydice, daughter of Elysium: truth and beauty meet
In the immortal word. Orpheus put his arms about his bride,
Clasped her, and folded her to timeless rest.
And so it came to pass as it had been foretold.
Today they walk together, side by side. Sometimes
He follows her; sometimes she follows him. However they
Move, wherever they go, Orpheus has no reason now
To look behind at her.

The Horned Owl

January is owl weather.
Old snow lies dingy,
Hard, frozen stiff, slick,
But there are also long, sharp cracks in the ice.
High up in the trees throughout the night
The eyes of the birds are open,
Blinking in pairs without eyelids,
Gleaming as they sit, still, on branches
In the dense black woods.

Every owl is awake, and it knows something:
It can feel it within its hollow bones,
The light bones of those that fly,
Empty bones, built-in barometers, conjuring sticks.
In this month of Janus, the two-headed
God of commencement, looking both
Forward and backwards, each owl is sage.
So each old bird winks as it looks over
Icicles that hang glistening,
Shining in the furrows of gray rocks.

The owls know the winter solstice is over;
In their feathers they feel the sun climbing breathless
The long, cold slope up the ecliptic,
Changing like old clothes the constellations,
Mounting the signs of the zodiac,
From the Goat through Aquarius and Pisces
Scaling the winter stars that will end up
Riding the Ram of March, in spring.

Time marches towards beginnings:
Check the length of the shadows at midday,
Watch the position of the sun at noon,
At night, listen to the owls——
Catch the turning of the year.
"Tu-whit, tu-who" rings out crisply clear
Shaking the frost in the winter dark
As the great horned owl
Ruffles the plumage on his thick neck,
Erects his soft feathers, and hoots.

Odin's Ride

    (Götterdammerung)

Where is the one in the golden helmet who'll ride
Over the wind and the water, climbing the knolls
Odin appearing triumphant to fight by our side
Now that Thor is away and thrashing the trolls?
The fortress of earth is surrounded by hostile tribes,
Its Midgard is cold beneath the boom of the sea;
Icy monsters sneering their horrible gibes
Are beating the fragile dykes of the mind into scree;
The Midgard-serpent is swimming in venomous stuff;
Chaos and Old Night are rising against the gods;
And no man can see further than Odin's meeting the Wolf.
So learn what we can; attack, whatever the odds,
In absolute courage, oblivious to every temptation,
Knowing that death and defeat are not refutation.

Ode for Carved Birds

How softly the mist rises from the lake today,
Gentling the contours of every shape and line
While taming all colors into varied shades of gray
Till there are no corners anywhere, no tine,
No tooth, nothing sharply branching pronged,
Every antlered horn of the masculine deer
Dociled as if the antelope world belonged
To the tender doe alone whose moist eyes veer
Bashfully behind a forest's leaf veneer.

Stretching their necks in the fog, etched black and white,
The Canada geese have turned bald blunt beaks west,
Pointing their heads to the wide ebbing of light,
Each bird in the same direction, each curved crest
Silhouetted edged like the geese carved flightless
On the wall of an Egyptian tomb's cut stone,
Encased in the obscure womb of the dead sightless,
Immortal sacred script incised in the bone
Of the rock, floating sinuous, hewn lone.

In files carved geese are striding their rhythmic row,
And the curve of the neck of each bird is shaped like an eye.
No need to decipher a Rosetta stone to know
That the symbol for the organ of seeing must testify
Behind all hieroglyphic night that identity
Is sight. Sound leaves echoes, its tones repeating,
But light, either on or off, is, reality
Revealed in each form giving a mummy its greeting:
Sagacity in each bird honed, death defeating.